WHEN THE TIME COMES TO BUY, YOU WON'T WANT TO

TIMELESS PIECES OF WIT AND WISDOM
COMPILED BY A WALL STREET LEGEND

This digital book is best viewed on a tablet.

ISBN: 978-0-9913682-8-0

Cover designed by BookCoverArt.webs.com
Cover photo by Wendy Dwyer

Interior design by Booknook.biz.

WHEN THE TIME COMES TO BUY, YOU WON'T WANT TO

TIMELESS PIECES OF WIT AND WISDOM
COMPILED BY A WALL STREET LEGEND

WALTER DEEMER

ALSO BY WALTER DEEMER

The Essential Basics of Technical Analysis

The Essential Basics of Technical Analysis for Financial Advisors

BY WALTER DEEMER AND SUSAN CRAGIN

Deemer on Technical Analysis

TO BOBBIE

Without her, where would I be...

INTRODUCTION

In the 1970's, when I was heading Putnam Investments' Market Analysis Department, the market started a correction. Happily, I had anticipated it.

Some of the permabull-money managers, who were generally skeptical of technical analysis in the first place, were annoyed that the market was going down as I had predicted. They started coming into my office almost immediately: "Is it time to buy yet?"

"No, not yet."

This went on day after day as the market kept going down, and I got tired of saying "No, not yet" over and over again. Finally, I shrugged my shoulders and said "When the time comes to buy, you won't want to".

* * * * * * * * * * * * * * * * * * * *

I worked with institutional money managers for over 50 years. I soon learned if I could make a point quickly and clearly it was a lot more likely to get into their decision-making process. That's why I've coined phrases like "When the time comes to buy, you won't want to" throughout my career; powerful messages conveyed in just a few words. I've also carefully curated them from the very talented people I've been fortunate to have been able to work with. This book is a compilation of the most perceptive and insightful phrases of all.

The book is divided into five sections: The Essential Basics, Technical Analysis, Psychology/Sentiment, Investing, and Potpourri. We'll start with the essential basics.

PART I

THE ESSENTIAL BASICS

"A stock is not the same as the company."

— WALTER DEEMER

You buy stocks, not companies. They're not the same thing.

Take a look at my favorite chart of all time on the next page: a monthly chart of McDonald's from 1970-1981. Both the stock price and the earnings per share are shown. The scales are set up so that when price is on top of the earnings line, the stock is selling at 15 times earnings. If the price is above it, the P/E's over 15; below it, less than 15.

The company did spectacularly well between 1972 and 1980; earnings grew at a compounded 25%/year. But investors don't buy companies, they buy stocks – and McDonald's stock ignored the company's sensational performance, declining over 50% during those eight years. The P/E ratio plummeted from 75 to 8 in the process.

A stock is not the same as the company.

The McDonald's saga is discussed at much greater length in *Deemer on Technical Analysis* – including the incredible tale of how Putnam, who bought the stock at its high in late 1972-early 1973, then sold it at its low in 1980.

That selling prevented me from recommending McDonalds, as I wanted to, when I was the special guest on *Wall $treet Week* on February 29, 1980.

I've treasured the interoffice memo that follows the chart ever since.

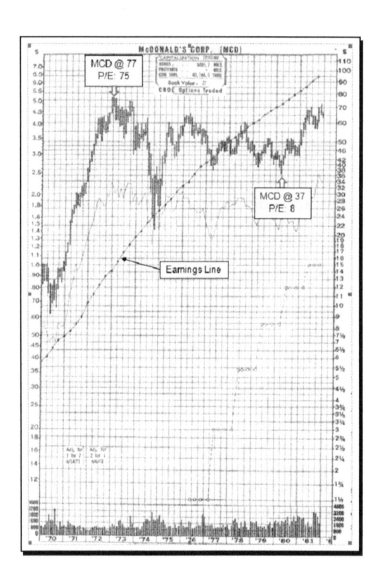

<u>I N T E R O F F I C E   M E M O R A N D U M</u>

TO: Norton H. Reamer, Martin M. Hale,
        J. David Wimberly, and Michael C. Hewitt

FROM: Walter R. Deemer   DATE: February 13, 1980

<u>GROWTH STOCKS</u>

As you know, I think that the big growth stocks are very attractive tech-
nically, with most of them apparently in the final phases of major reversal
patterns. I also think that when the long-delayed recession finally hits that
their earnings gains during a period of generally declining profits will make
them stand out like "beacons in the night."

Two of the most obvious, at least to me, are McDonald's and Philip Morris,
(which presently happen to be selling at 9 and 8 times trailing earnings, respec-
tively) and I thought that it might be nice to mention them on the Wall Street
Week program if the subject should come up. However, on checking with the
Advisory Company, I was told I couldn't--they have sell programs underway presently
in both stocks.

If this isn't a major buy signal for growth stocks, I don't know what is;
the stocks are apparently being sold because of their disappointing price performance, but from a technical point of view, I think it's wrong to sell them now.

WRD

"The stock market is not the same as the economy."

— WALTER DEEMER

The macro form of "A stock is not the same as the company". Let economists do the economic analysis.

"The stock market is a better economic forecaster than economists."

— **WALTER DEEMER**

The stock market is a leading economic indicator. It turns up and down – quite reliably – before the economy does.

Economists don't have nearly as good a record.

*"The stock market has forecast nine
of the last five recessions."*

— PAUL SAMUELSON

Professor Samuelson's snarky remark nevertheless has an important message for investors: Many bear markets are <u>not</u> associated with a recession.

(It's now thirteen of the last seven, by the way.)

"Price is everything!"

— WALTER DEEMER

You don't buy earnings.

You don't buy dividends.

You don't buy management.

You buy stocks. And you buy them at a price certain.

And when you go to sell, you don't sell earnings, dividends or management; you sell stocks. And you sell them at a price certain.

Price is everything.

"Price is never adjusted."

— SAM STOVALL, CFRP

"Technical analysis is the most basic part of investment analysis."

— WALTER DEEMER

You buy stocks, not companies.

Technical analysis is what you use to analyze stocks.

Q. E. D.

"All price changes are caused by an imbalance in supply and demand."

— WALTER DEEMER

A price change occurs because of – and only because of – an imbalance in supply and demand (although the media and Internet folks will consume enormous amounts of energy to explain why it happened).

"The stock market is not a random walk; people react to every price change."

— JOHN SCHULZ
(BREAN MURRAY;
FORBES COLUMNIST)

John Schulz observed back in the 1970's that price moves are not random, as many professors allege, because each and every price change evokes some sort of response from market participants. In a "random walk", the moves are completely independent from each other.

(For those who wish to dig deeper, see Chapter 2 of *Deemer on Technical Analysis*. There's also a picture of me, as President of the Market Technicians Association, presenting Mr. Schulz with the MTA's Annual Award in 1977 for his lifetime achievements in the field of technical analysis.)

*"A picture is worth 1000 words —
and a chart is worth 1000 numbers."*

— **WALTER DEEMER**

"The two most important things on a stock chart are price and relative strength."

— **WALTER DEEMER**

Price tells you whether the stock is going up or down.

Relative strength tells you whether the stock is going up or down faster or slower than the market itself.

There are only four possible combinations, as discussed in Chapter 6 of *"The Basic Essentials of Technical Analysis"*:

Up/Up. The best of all possible worlds.

Up/Down. Not terrible; you're making money, but just not keeping up with the market.

Down/Up. Not great; you're losing money, but at least not as much as most people.

Down/Down. The worst of all possible worlds.

"I never look at a chart that doesn't have a relative strength line on it."

— DAVE KELLER
(FIDELITY)

How important is relative strength?

That's how important the recently-retired head of Fidelity's Technical Department thinks it is.

*"Relative strength in a
bear market sucks!"*

— WALTER DEEMER

Losing less money than a benchmark means you're still losing money.

PART II

TECHNICAL ANALYSIS

*"There is more human intelligence
focused on the corner of Broad and
Wall than any other place on
the planet."*

— RICHARD RUSSELL

Stock prices are determined by an incredible number of buyers and sellers all over the world who use an infinite number of factors of constantly-changing significance to arrive at their buy and sell decisions. We use technical analysis to study the net result.

It's a noble mission.

Note: The late Richard Russell penned this back when The New York Stock Exchange, at the corner of Broad and Wall Streets in Lower Manhattan, represented the entire stock market.

"The market is the wisdom of all investors."

— ALEC YOUNG
(FTSE RUSSELL)

"Always remember that we are dealing with probabilities and not certainties."

— G. STANLEY BERGE
(TUCKER ANTHONY)

This is one of the most important ones of all; <u>nothing</u> in the stock market is <u>ever</u> a 100% certainty.

"Tops are a process and bottoms are an event."

— DOUG KASS
(SEABREEZE PARTNERS)

"They don't ring a bell at the top."

———————

— UNKNOWN

"The market gets most oversold at a bottom and most overbought at the beginning of an advance."

— WALTER DEEMER

"Markets (and stocks) can stay overbought for a long time if the advance is really strong."

— WALTER DEEMER

The stronger the advance the bigger the initial overbought condition and the longer it lasts – and when the market gets really, really overbought it generates the Breakaway Momentum that heralds a new bull market.

(You can learn about Breakaway Momentum – a concept I developed in 1973 -- at https://www. walterdeemer.com/bam.htm.)

Author's Note: The market generated Breakaway Momentum on January 9, 2019, just as I was completing this book.

"The most bullish thing the market can do is get overbought and stay so."

— CHUCK SPETH/JOHN BOLLINGER

"If everyone's waiting for a pullback to buy, either the market doesn't have a pullback or, if it does, you shouldn't buy into it."

———————————

— BOB FARRELL
(MERRILL LYNCH)

(A deep bow to legendary Merrill Lynch market analyst Bob Farrell, my greatest mentor.)

"If you need an indicator to tell you whether sentiment is extreme, it's not."

— WALTER DEEMER

"If you need an indicator to tell you whether speculative activity is dangerously high, it's not."

— WALTER DEEMER

"No indicator speaks all the time."

— JOHN BOLLINGER

"Watch their feet, not their mouths."

— **WALTER DEEMER**

Look at what investors are doing rather than their opinions.

"Margin clerks are the most ruthless sellers Wall Street has ever known."

— JOHN MENDELSON
(MORGAN STANLEY)

When margin clerks are told to sell, they sell immediately – at any price they can get. That's why so many bottoms are accompanied by some sort of forced selling.

"Parabolic advances usually carry further than you think, but they do not correct by going sideways."

— BOB FARRELL
(MERRILL LYNCH)

You have to be able to see the parabolic advance on a semi-log (ratio) chart, though. Parabolic advances on arithmetic charts don't count.

"What is <u>not</u> happening can be more important than what is."

— MARK DIBBLE
(FIDELITY)

PART III

PSYCHOLOGY/ SENTIMENT

"When the time comes to buy, you won't want to."

— WALTER DEEMER

Sentiment is pervasively bearish at and just after a significant stock market bottom; the gloom is thick enough to cut with a knife. When the time comes to buy, then, you have to fly in the face of the overwhelmingly-pervasive bearishness, screw up your courage, and buy.

The stock market is a cruel mistress.

*"When the time comes to sell,
you won't want to do that, either."*

— WALTER DEEMER

"Nobody knows how traumatic a test of a low is until they've lived through one."

———————————

— WALTER DEEMER

Especially since not all of them are successful.

"There are no atheists in bear markets."

— WALTER DEEMER

*"An investor's four biggest enemies
are Hope, Greed, Fear and Vanity."*

— REMINISCENCES OF A
STOCK OPERATOR (EDWIN LEFÈVRE)

A timeless observation from the best book ever written
on the psychology of trading.

*"When everybody thinks alike,
everyone is likely to be wrong."*

— HUMPHREY NEILL

Contrary Opinion, as defined by its originator and best-known proponent.

"The stock market will do whatever it has to do to embarrass the greatest number of people to the greatest extent possible."

— **WALTER DEEMER**

Deemer's Law Of Perversity; a vicious, nasty step beyond contrary opinion.

"It ain't when everyone turns bearish that's important — it's when they finish selling."

— WALTER DEEMER

"We have nothing to fear but the lack of fear itself."

———

— WALTER DEEMER

"Bull markets climb a wall of worry. Bear markets slide down a slope of hope."

— OLD WALL STREET ADAGE

"Nothing generates bullish sentiment more than a powerful, relentless advance."

— WALTER DEEMER

And nothing generates bearish sentiment more than a powerful, relentless decline. (H/T to Helene Meisler.)

"In bull markets stocks don't go down on bad news. In bear markets stocks don't go up on good news."

— HAROLD EHRLICH
(BERNSTEIN-MACAULAY)

"A bull market is when you check your stocks every day to see how much they went up. A bear market is when you don't bother to look any more."

— JOHN HAMMERSLOUGH
(KAUFMANN ALSBERG)

*"Just when you find the key
to the market, they change
the locks."*

— G<small>ERALD</small> L<small>OEB</small>,
E. F. H<small>UTTON</small> (1955)

Sisyphus is the patron saint of market analysts.

"When a trader starts to feel really smart, he/she is headed for a huge drawdown."

— PETER BRANDT **(2018)**

Gerald Loeb's classic quote updated by a legendary futures trader.

PART IV

INVESTING

*"If it sounds too good to be true,
it almost certainly is."*

— WALTER DEEMER

Memo to people who assure us they can outperform the market each and every year, tell us they can deliver a guaranteed riskless return well above the going rate, etc., etc., etc.

It can't be done.

"More money has been lost reaching for yield than at the point of a gun."

— RAY DEVOE
(SPENCER TRASK)

When someone is hawking "risk-free investments" with yields well above Treasury rates, red flags are flying. Those "risk-free investments" aren't risk-free at all.

"The four costliest words in financial markets are 'This time is different'."

— WALTER DEEMER

"Extremely crowded trades rarely work extremely well."

— WALTER DEEMER

An extremely crowded trade is when everyone on Wall Street "knows" something's a sure thing and piles into it.

There are no sure things on Wall Street, and extremely crowded trades have a nasty habit of blowing up rather spectacularly at some point.

"Better or worse matters more than good or bad."

— LIZ ANN SONDERS
(SCHWAB)

Bad but getting better is a whole lot different than bad but getting worse.

"No stock in an uptrend has ever gone bankrupt."

— **WALTER DEEMER**

"I'm glad the stock didn't go down in vain."

— WALTER DEEMER

It was during a morning investment meeting at Putnam. The market looked like it was bottoming but GM had just cut its dividend. The stock had already declined from the 70's to the low 40's and was set to open even lower, but some of the fund managers still wanted to sell it. I took a look at the chart and, sure enough, GM also looked like it was bottoming. So I piped up: "I'm glad the stock didn't go down in vain."

"What?"

"The stock has already fallen 30 points. It didn't go down for no reason."

Bad news often materializes at the end of a decline.

"There's no such thing as a "one-decision" stock."

— WALTER DEEMER

In the early 1970's, consumer growth stocks were all the rage. They were called "one-decision" stocks because the only decision investors had to make was to buy them; their growth would continue forever.

As you saw from the McDonalds chart, that didn't end up too well.

One-decision stocks surface in every bull market. The most recent examples are the "FAANG" stocks (Facebook, Amazon, Apple, Netflix and Google).

Like every one-decision stock during the past 100 years, though, even the FAANGs won't go up forever.

And when the time comes to sell, you won't want to.

"Financial stocks are the canaries in the stock market coal mine."

— WALTER DEEMER

Financial stocks usually turn up or down ahead of the rest of the market. Furthermore, financial market stresses almost always surface in financial stocks before the rest of the market.

(H/T to Joe Generalis, then at Oppenheimer, who taught me that financial stocks were a leading indicator in the early 1970's.)

*"Commodity stocks tend to turn up
and down before the underlying
commodity."*

— JOHN MAURICE (PUTNAM)

"There's no fever like gold fever."

— RICHARD RUSSELL

"Never confuse your views with what is actually happening in the stock market."

— @TRADERSTEWIE

PART V

POTPOURRI

"Don't keep checking prices all the time just because you can."

— **WALTER DEEMER**

It's tempting – but if you do, you're in grave danger of losing an essential part of what makes a successful investor.

Long-term perspective.

*"There are lines between investing
and speculating and between
speculating and gambling,
but I have no idea where they are."*

— WALTER DEEMER

There are elements of speculation in investing, and there are elements of gambling in speculation.

I have no idea where the lines of demarcation are.

"All of us have a 'Shoulda Fund'.
Don't waste time obsessing over it."

— **WALTER DEEMER**

At Putnam, fund managers would often grumble "I shoulda bought that". Or "I shoulda sold that".

I told them to put it in the Putnam Shoulda Fund. It was the best-performing fund we ever had.

Learning from mistakes is good – but obsessing over them is a waste of time. Just put them in your Shoulda Fund and move on.

"If you want to watch CNBC like the pros do, turn the sound off!"

— WALTER DEEMER

Seriously. I have been in trading rooms and offices of all shapes and sizes. All of them had CNBC on – but they always had it muted.

They're watching it for breaking news, not the non-stop parade of talking heads uttering opinions they're never held accountable for.

(A personal aside: During a presentation at the 2000 MTA Seminar in Atlanta, I presented – very much tongue-in-cheek – items our South Florida chapter was "selling" in a "fundraiser". One of them was a big sign for people to hold up at the beginning of a CNBC appearance: "TURN THE SOUND UP". John Bollinger asked me to give him the sign afterwards, but I don't know if he ever actually used it.)

"Those who cannot remember the past are condemned to repeat it."

— GEORGE SANTAYANA

*"History doesn't repeat itself,
but it often rhymes."*

— MARK TWAIN (?)

"The stock market is the creation of man that has most humbled him."

— ALAN SHAW
(SMITH BARNEY HARRIS UPHAM)

"The way to make money in the stock market is to find a good stock and buy it. When it goes up, sell it. If it don't go up, don't buy it."

— WILL ROGERS

Res ipsa loquitor.

PART VI

BENEDICTION

"Price Is Everything!"

A NOTE FROM THE AUTHOR

Dear Reader:

I hope this collection of "perceptive phrases" has given you the same valuable insights into investor psychology and how financial markets work as they have me.

I've posted some of them previously on Twitter. If you'd like to see new ones, you can follow me there: @ walterdeemer. (Yes, I know, it's Twitter – but by carefully selecting who to follow you can get a lot of surprisingly useful information there.)

In the meantime, many thanks for reading – and my sincere wishes for profitable investing in the future!

– Walter Deemer

ABOUT THE AUTHOR

Walter Deemer retired in 2016 after a 52-year career as a market analyst. He worked for Merrill Lynch and Tsai Management and Research in New York and Putnam Investments in Boston before striking out on his own in 1980. He graduated from Penn State with honors in 1963 and has been aggressively continuing his education in the School of Hard Knocks ever since. He has been married to his wife, Bobbie, for 45 years. They moved into the independent wing of a senior living facility in Stuart, Florida two years ago, where he enjoys watching the market and maintaining an impish presence on Twitter.

— **Diane Gallagher, DSG Designs**

19957494R00055